A POSTCARD
FROM THE
CONWY

JAN DOBRZYNSKI & KEITH TURNER

The
History
Press

First published 2010

The History Press
The Mill, Brimscombe Port
Stroud, Gloucestershire, GL5 2QG
www.thehistorypress.co.uk

British Library Cataloguing in Publication Data.
A catalogue record for this book is available from the British Library.

ISBN 978 0 7524 5458 0
Typesetting and origination by The History Press
Printed in Great Britain
Manufacturing managed by Jellyfish Print Solutions Ltd

Contents

Introduction   5

1.   The Young River   7

2.   The Lledr   15

3.   Betws-y-Coed   25

4.   The Llugwy   41

5.   The Lower River   65

6.   Conwy Town   89

7.   Into the Bay   113

> Conway, which out of his streame doth send
> Plenty of pearles to deck his dames withall
>
> (*The Faerie Queene*, Edmund Spenser)

In past centuries, Afon Conwy mussels were an important source of freshwater pearls – examples of which, or so legend has it, can be seen today in the British Crown Jewels.

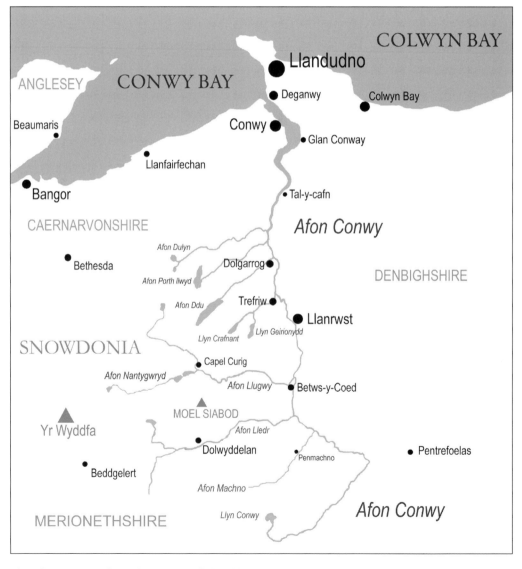

The Afon Conwy and its tributaries (with the old county names).

Introduction

Although not one of Britain's longest rivers, the Afon Conwy – or River Conwy (formerly Conway) in English – more than makes up in spectacle and landscape beauty what it may lack in simple miles. Rising in the eastern highlands of North Wales (its small source lake being Llyn Conwy), the young river cascades in a northerly direction towards the tourist honeypot of Betws-y-Coed, collecting from the west its two major tributaries, the Lledr and the Llugwy, to the south and the north of the village respectively. (Both these rivers are featured here, and deservedly so as they are inseparable parts of the story of both the Conwy and Betws-y-Coed.)

Leaving the charms of Betws-y-Coed behind, the river continues its northerly course, though now at a far gentler pace as its valley opens up, through Llanrwst and on to the historic town of Conwy. Here, between the town's ancient quayside (from where, legend has it, Prince Madog set sail to discover North America) and the far more ancient Great Orme headland, the river joins the Irish Sea in Conwy Bay, its journey of some 30 miles.

The Conwy's setting in the topography of North Wales has, down the centuries, afforded it an importance far beyond its size: firstly as a military gateway into the heart of North Wales – for the conquering Roman Legions and then the armies of England as they attempted to subdue the Welsh peoples – and secondly, in later, more peaceful times, as a seemingly impassable barrier which, together with the mountains of Snowdonia immediately to its west, has, from Roman times to the recent past, severely impeded the progress of travellers from England to Ireland via Anglesey. Some of the ways in which this obstacle has been overcome, and the river's more benign role from the late eighteenth century onwards as a tourist attraction in its own right, will be seen in many of the postcards reproduced here as they take the reader on a journey in words and pictures down the Conwy all the way from its headwaters to the sea. It is a record of soaring mountains and tranquil lakes, majestic bridges and castles, humble sailboats and Edwardian pleasure steamers – all immortalised by past generations of photographers and artists for the benefit of innumerable tourists and travellers.

All the postcards included in this book are from the authors' collections. Publication details are given at the end of the captions exactly as they appear on the cards.

For various reasons, the spelling of many Welsh place names has varied somewhat over the past hundred years or so. Unless quoted in context otherwise, the modern versions of all place names have been used in the text.

A wonderful advertising postcard for Bass Pale Ale, with twelve tiny fold-out views of Conwy hidden inside the bottle. (Similar cards would have been overprinted for sale in other seaside towns.) In the world of advertising, the familiar red triangle on the Bass bottle is famous for being the first ever Registered Trade Mark and until comparatively recent times it was one of the most recognisable beer logos around. (*Message Novelty Card The Photochrom Co. Ltd London and Tunbridge Wells*)

1

The Young River

I crossed a bridge over a river, which, brawling and tumbling amidst rocks, shaped its course to the north-east. As I proceeded, the country became more and more wild; there were dingles and hollows in abundance, and fantastic-looking hills, some of which were bare, and others clad with trees of various kinds.

(*Wild Wales*, George Borrow, 1857)

The paddle steamer *Prince George* making its way up the Conwy towards Trefriw, on the tide. Launched as the *New St George* at Amlwch on Anglesey in 1891, she was 72ft in length, had a gross tonnage of 24 tons and was licensed to carry 190 passengers. Owned and operated by the St George Steamship Co., she was renamed *Prince George* in 1910 and withdrawn for scrapping in 1936. (*T.R. Hammond, Conway*)

Near Conway Falls, Betws-y-Coed

The young Afon Conwy, above Betws-y-Coed, tumbling down the Conwy Falls in its narrow, steep-sided, wooded valley. The falls are a haven for wildlife, including otters and dippers, while the surrounding woods are home to the green and the greater spotted woodpecker. (*T. Edwards, 50 Eccleston St., Prescot*)

Conway Falls, Bettws-y-Coed

Still very young, it is here, at the picturesque Conwy Falls immediately below where the river is joined by the waters of the Afon Machno, that the Conwy shows the first facet of its distinctive character. The falls are but a few yards from the A5 and can be reached from the car park next to the Otter Restaurant and Café – designed by Sir Clough Williams-Ellis and painted pink to accord with his buildings at Portmeirion. *(Publisher unidentified)*

The Conwy Falls again with, running up from the lower right, its Victorian salmon ladder installed to help salmon (and trout) gain the higher reaches of the river in order to spawn. The ladder has since been superseded by a subterranean fish pass of 25 linked pools, with the Environment Agency Wales electronically monitoring the size and species of fish using it. *(Valentine's Series)*

Below the falls the character of the river changes, becoming more peaceful as its valley widens a little and its headlong rush slows down. *(Judges Ltd. Hastings)*

Immediately above Betws-y-Coed the Conwy reverts, briefly, to its younger self as it gushes through the dramatic Fairy Glen. *(E.T.W. Dennis & Sons Ltd., London & Scarborough)*

The Fairy Glen again, its semi-magical nature captured perfectly by the camera. *(Collotype Postcard Picture by Judges' Ltd., Hastings)*

A most unusual card, apparently composed of a private family photograph mounted on the peeled-off back of an unidentified foreign postcard. The sender's message, dated 7 October 1906, reads, 'Hope you will like this P.C.; it is a view I took at Bettws-y-Coed (Fairy Glen). The card is one you gave me some time ago and I thought I would experiment on it.'

The Fairy Glen again, this time with a lone, pensive figure to give a sense of scale – and drama – to the scene. *(The Star Series – G.D. & D., London)*

Fairy Glen looking down Bettws-y-coed   70/2

A final look at Fairy Glen, with the river departing northwards to meet the Afon Lledr. The card was sent from Peterborough to Oundle in Northamptonshire in 1911 – presumably someone's holiday souvenir employed to send a mundane message to a friend. *(The British Mirror Series)*

2

The Lledr

The extension of the railway from Bettws-y-Coed to the slate districts of Festiniog is now in progress. The new line passes through the valley of the Lledwr, by Dolwyddelan Castle, said to be have been the birthplace of Llewylyn the Great.

(*The Official Tourists' Picturesque Guide*, London & North Western Railway Co., 1876)

(Judges' Ltd Hastings)

Crimea Pass, or Bwlch y Gorddinan, on the upper reaches of the Lledr above Roman Bridge. The use of 'Crimea' in British place names dates back to the Crimean War of the mid-nineteenth century and was adopted to signify the isolation (and coldness) of a particular spot. In this particular instance it took its name from the Crimea Inn at the 1,263ft summit of the pass, so named after the war being fought when the road was constructed. *(Valentine's)*

The bridge after which the settlement of Roman Bridge is named, on a publicity postcard issued by the London & North Western Railway whose branch line from Llandudno Junction to Blaenau Ffestiniog ran up the Conwy and Lledr valleys. A printed message on the back of the card exhorts the purchaser to, 'Visit North Wales for a Charming Holiday. Picturesque Scenery. Grand Mountain Views. Waterfalls. Lakes. Popular Seaside Attractions. Excellent Hotels and Boarding Houses.' *(McCorquodale & Co., Limited)*

Commanding the north side of the Lledr Valley below Roman Bridge are the ruins of Dolwyddelan Castle. Dating back to about 1170, the castle was possibly built by Iorwerth, father of Llywelyn the Great, and was later captured (1283) and strengthened by Edward I as part of his military campaign to subdue the Welsh people. *(Judges' Ltd., Hastings)*

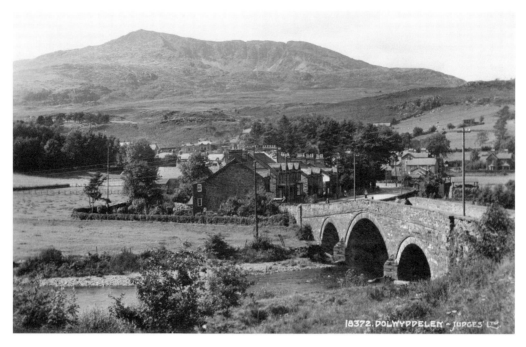

As the Lledr continues its journey eastwards, it reaches the village of Dolwyddelan where it is crossed by a minor road leading to the railway station. The distinctive peak on the skyline is that of Moel Siabod, rising to 2,861ft above sea level. *(Judges' Ltd., Hastings)*

Dolwyddelen.

BENAR VIEW HOTEL, DOLWYDDELEN.

This House is picturesquely situated in the Vale of Dolwyddelen,
being 6 miles fron the Railway Station, Bettws-y-coed.

A Handsome Coffee-Room, a Drawing-Room up-stairs, and Private Sitting-Rooms.
Excellent Trout and Salmon Fishing.   The River is well preserved, and Tickets can be obtained at the Hotel.

POSTING IN ALL ITS BRANCHES.
MODERATE CHARGES.
THOMAS T. WILLIAMS, Proprietor.

An advertisement for the now defunct Benar View Hotel at Dolwyddelan, taken from the 1877 *Gossiping Guide to Wales*. As will be seen in similar examples later, hotels in this whole area of North Wales were keen to advertise the facilities offered to anglers.

A general view of the Lledr Valley below Dolwyddelan on a 1936-franked postcard, looking back upstream with the former LNWR line from Betws-y-Coed to Blaenau Ffestiniog prominent on the southern bank on its approach to Bertheos Tunnel and Roman Bridge station. *(Raphael Tuck & Sons, Ltd)*

Another view of the valley, this time looking across it towards Moel Siabod. *(Valentine's Series)*

A similar view, but with what is now the (widened) A470 on the right, high on the northern bank of the river away from any danger of flooding. The field on the left is Lloes-y-Coed or 'Field in the Wood'. *(Valentine's)*

The next settlement (and railway station) down the Lledr is Pont-y-Pant, where the valley narrows abruptly as the mountains close in. *(A.E. Williams, Llandudno, Craig-y-don & Bettws-y-coed)*

The bridge –'pont' in Welsh – Pont-y-Pant, looking upstream from immediately below it. The sender's message, in 1932, reads, 'We are now staying at a little village called Dolwyddelan. We are on a day tour through Lledr valley. We are thoroughly enjoying ourselves & shall have a lot to tell you when we return. The weather today is grand.' *(Judges' Ltd., Hastings)*

Bettws-y-Coed,

PONT-Y-PANT HOTEL,

NEAR BETTWS-Y-COED,

JOHN JONES, PROPRIETOR.

CHOICE WINES,
Spirits, Ale, Beer, Porter, Lemonade, Soda Water, and Ginger Beer.

WELL-AIRED BEDS.

Good Stabling and Cars to Hire.

Adjoining the Hotel good Trout and Salmon Fishing.

An advertisement for the Pont-y-Pant Hotel – still very much in business today – from the 1877 *Gossiping Guide to Wales* again. The fact that the hotel makes a feature of its 'well-aired beds' speaks volumes for some of the rival establishments in the area!

Pont-y-Pant bridge again, this time from immediately above it. *(R Parry, Chemist, Bettws-y-Coed)*

The same view of the bridge but on a 1905-franked 'moonlight effect' postcard. Similar cards were produced by many publishers and were intended to emphasise the romantic nature of a particular beauty spot or landscape. *(S. Hildesheimer & Co., Ldt* [sic], *London & Manchester)*

Just before reaching Betws-y-Coed, the Lledr passes under another minor road bridge – known prosaically as the Lledr Bridge – linking the A470 on its northern bank with the scattered farms and cottages on its southern. *(The Woodbury Series)*

The Lledr Bridge again: another romanticised view, this time executed as an oil painting. *(Bettws-y-Coed Series S. Hildesheimer & Co, Ltd. London & Manchester)*

Here, on the southern edge of Betws-y-Coed, the Lledr tumbles into the broader waters of the young Afon Conwy. *(K Ltd)*

3

Betws-y-Coed

[. . .] or the 'Chapel' or the 'Station in the Wood', is a hamlet forming a romantic sylvan retreat, delightfully situated in the junction of the counties of Denbigh and Caernarvon, and a favourite haunt of anglers and artists.

(The Official Tourists' Picturesque Guide, London & North Western Railway Co., 1876)

(English Series Photo-Precision Ltd., St. Albans)

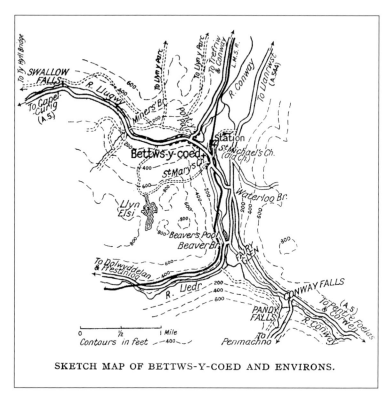

SKETCH MAP OF BETTWS-Y-COED AND ENVIRONS.

General map of Betws-y-Coed, as printed in a Ward, Lock & Co. Ltd *Guide to Colwyn Bay and North Wales* of the 1950s.

An overall view of Betws-y-Coed and its setting, looking northwards with the railway station, opened by the LNWR in 1868 as Bettws-y-Coed and renamed in 1953 with the modern spelling of the name, right of centre. (In the past it has also been timetabled as Bettws-y-Coed for Capel Curig to entice more passengers to use it, even though that village is 6 miles away.) Off to the left, behind the dark trees, is the valley of the Llugwy. *(Valentine's Series)*

General View, Bettws-y-Coed.

Another look down on Betws-y-Coed, on a 1914-franked postcard. This time the view is to the south, with the Afon Conwy and the railway station on the far left and the Llugwy Valley coming in from the right. *(A.E. Vollam, Llandudno, Craig-y-don, Bettws-y-Coed)*

5372 BETTWS-Y-COED: FROM MOUNT GARMON

The village again, looking down from a viewpoint on the heights of Mount Garmon westwards across the river and railway line to the Llugwy Valley. *(Photochrom Co., Ltd., London and Tunbridge Wells)*

Less than a mile south of Betws-y-Coed, roughly equidistant from the Conwy, the Lledr and the Llugwy, is the small lake Llyn Elsi, used since 1914 as a reservoir to supply water to the village when a 20ft dam was built to increase its capacity. Situated some 700ft above sea level, its waters were also employed to drive an early hydro-electric plant to power the village's lights. *(Publisher unidentified)*

Llyn Elsi again, with the stone commemorating the decision of Lord Ancaster, the local landowner, to give permission for the construction of the dam (and so form one lake from the small Llyn Rhisgog and Llyn Enoc). The lake is currently stocked with trout by a local angling club. *(Valentine's Series)*

Probably the most famous landmark in Betws-y-Coed is the Waterloo Bridge, carrying the Holyhead Road – now the A5 – over the Afon Conwy immediately south of the town. *(The Milton "Glazette" Series, Woolstone Bros, London E.C.)*

A closer view of the Waterloo Bridge. The work of Thomas Telford, it is so named because, as the lettering on the arch proclaims, it was constructed in the same year – 1815 – as the Battle of Waterloo. *(Photochrom Co. Ltd., London & Tunbridge Wells)*

A delightful view of the bridge from the roadway, probably in the 1920s, showing both a lack of vehicular traffic unimaginable today and that, despite the tourist trade, the economy of this part of North Wales was based then on agriculture. *(Valentine's)*

A little way north of the Waterloo Bridge is the railway station, sandwiched between the A5 and the west bank of the Conwy. (See also pp. 26 and 27.) Alongside it today is the Conwy Valley Railway Museum complete with a miniature railway and tramway offering rides to visitors. *(G.R. Thompson, the Post Card King, Llandudno)*

Betws-y-Coed's first parish church, dedicated to St Michael and reputed to be one of the oldest in Wales, dating as it does from at least the fourteenth century. *(Peacock Brand. "Autochrom" (Colour Photo) Postcard, Pictorial Stationery Co. Ltd., London)*

The old church again, on the west bank of the Conwy close to the railway station. It was superseded in the nineteenth century by St Mary's Church on the A5 opposite the station, and now functions just as a cemetery. *(Valentine's XL Series)*

London and North Western Railway.

TOURS THROUGH SNOWDON DISTRICT, 1877.

Arrangements have been made with the Coach Proprietors for a series of Coach Tours through the Snowdon District, in connection with the London and North Western Co.'s trains from Chester, Rhyl, Llandudno, Bangor, Carnarvon, &c. Passengers at the time of starting in the morning are furnished with tickets, which ensure their being provided with seats on the Coaches. The following are particulars of the routes of the various tours.

TOUR No. 1.—By Rail to Llanberis, thence by Coach through the "Pass of Llanberis," and past the Swallow Waterfall to Bettwsycoed, and by Rail home to the Station from which the Tourist started in the morning.

TOUR No. 2.—By Rail to Bettwsycoed, thence through same District as No. 1 Tour to Llanberis. Home by Train.

TOUR No. 3.—By Rail to Carnarvon, thence by Coach round Snowdon to Beddgelert, and through the Vale of Gwynant, and the Pass of Llanberis to Carnarvon. Home by Train.

TOUR No. 4.—By Rail to Bettwsycoed, thence by Coach past the Swallow Waterfalls, Capel Curig, the Vale of Nant Francon, and the Penrhyn Slate Quarries to Bangor. Home by Train, and vice versa.

TOUR No. 5.—By Rail to Llanberis, thence by Coach to Beddgelert, and back to Llanberis. Home by Train.

TOUR No. 6.—By Rail to Bettwsycoed, thence by Coach to Beddgelert, and back to Bettwsycoed. Home by Train.

TOUR No. 7.—By Rail to Bettwsycoed, thence by Coach to the Fairy Glen, Conway Falls, Pandy Mill Falls, and along the Pentre Voelas Road as far as Voelas Hall, and back to Bettwsycoed. Home by Train.

These Routes cover some of the most beautiful scenery in North Wales. Full particulars as to the fares, times of starting, &c., can be obtained from the Special Bills which are issued, and which may be obtained at any of the Principal Stations and Hotels along the North Wales Coast.

TOURIST ARRANGEMENTS.

First, Second, and Third Class Tourist Tickets, available for Two Calendar Months, will be issued from May 14th to October 31st inclusive, at the Principal Stations on the London and North-Western Railway, to places of interest and attraction in the United Kingdon.

PIC-NIC AND PLEASURE PARTIES.

From May 1st to October 31st inclusive, First, Second, and Third Class Return Tickets will (with certain limitations) be issued at Reduced Fares to Parties of not less than six first or ten second or third class passengers. Application to be made at any of the Stations at least three days before the date of the proposed excursion.

CHEAP RETURN TICKETS.

Return Tickets at Cheap Fares are issued from Birmingham, Liverpool, Manchester, Warrington, &c., to the principal places of attraction in North Wales, on Saturdays, available for return on the following Monday.

Any information as to Tourist and Pleasure Party arrangements, Excursion Trains, &c., can be obtained on application to E. M. G. Eddy, London and North-Western Railway, Chester, G. P. Neele, Euston Station, London, or to the undersigned,

G. FINDLAY.

Chief Traffic Manager's Office,
Euston Station, London.

The Conwy Valley was very much London & North Western Railway 'territory' and the company made the most of the fact by promoting a variety of tours and excursions in the area, as for example these listed in their advertisement in the 1877 *Gossiping Guide to Wales*.

In the heart of Betws-y-Coed: the High Street, then as now renowned for its picturesque appearance and a magnet for artists and photographers. *(The Wrench Series)*

The High Street again. The printed legend on the reverse of the card exhorts the reader to 'Buy Your Boots from Sterlings Ltd, The Famous Family Booters.' *(Ashtons' Southport. Grosvenor Series)*

A postcard issued to promote the former Tanlan Temperance Hotel in Betws-y-Coed, and presumably sold (or given away) to guests. Similar cards are still published today for hotels and pubs, though temperance hotels are now very much a thing of the past. *(Publisher unidentified)*

Another hotel postcard, this time of the non-advertising variety. The Royal Oak is still very much in business today as one of the premier hotels of the region. *(Valentine's Series)*

The Royal Oak again, in its glorious setting on the A5 and the Afon Llugwy. *(English Series, Photo-Precision Ltd., St. Albans)*

The Llugwy from the grounds of the Royal Oak Hotel, on a 1908-franked postcard, looking eastwards to the village. *(Publisher unidentified)*

On the Conwy below St Michael's Church is the Church Pool, where the river widens and becomes more tranquil again. *(S. Hildesheimer & Co., Ltd, London & Manchester. Views of North Wales)*

This footbridge, known as the Sappers' Suspension Bridge, spans the Afon Conwy carrying a footpath from the A470 on the eastern bank of the river to St Michael's Church and the railway station on the western. It derives its name from the fact that it was built in the 1930s by sappers – Royal Engineers – to replace a wooden bridge that had been destroyed by storms and so reconnect their army camp in the east-bank meadows with the village. *("Phototype" Postcard. Valentine & Sons, Ltd., Dundee and London)*

The famous stepping-stones by the old church. According to the printed legend on the reverse of the card, 'The Stepping Stones across the river are, even since the construction of the various bridges, a favourite method of crossing the waters of the River Conway. The scenery at this point is most delightful, the beauties of rock, stream, hills and trees combining to form one of the daintiest series of landscapes that the vicinity of Bettws-y-Coed provides and consequently the Stepping Stones are greatly favoured by artists.' *(S. Hildesheimer & Co., Ltd. London & Manchester. Views of North Wales)*

Another highly romanticised image, from a painting by E. Longstaffe, of the stepping-stones, complete with children, a horseman, and a solitary angler. The card was posted in 1939. *(Raphael Tuck & Sons' "Oilette" Postcard)*

A far more realistic view of the stepping-stones in as much as it is a real photographic postcard – though the romanticism, in the shape of the trio of artfully posed young girls, is just as evident. *(Publisher unidentified)*

Almost every beauty spot has to have a place of outdoor refreshment, and Betws-y-Coed was no exception. These are the Riverside Tea Gardens, by the stepping-stones, with a gardener mowing the immaculate lawn. On the right is what appears to be an equally immaculate bowling green. *(Photochrom Co. Ltd., London and Tunbridge Wells)*

This 1923-franked card continues the angling theme, with a photograph of a fly-fisherman testing his skill below Betws-y-Coed. *(Publisher unidentified)*

To close the chapter, a postcard of a type that appears very odd to modern eyes but was quite common during the years before, during and after the First World War: a sunny scene overprinted for use as a Christmas card. *(The L.P. & F.A.P. Llandrindod Wells)*

4

The Llugwy

First there are a number of little foaming torrents, bursting through rocks about twenty yards above the promontory . . . then there is a swirl of water round its corner into a pool below on its right, black as death and seemingly of great depth; then a rush through a very narrow outlet into another pool, from which the water clamours away down the glen. Such is the Rhaiadr y Wennol, or Swallow Fall [. . .]

(Wild Wales, George Borrow, 1857)

("Phototype" Postcard. Valentine & Sons, Ltd., Dundee & London)

The Afon Llugwy rises in the high moorlands to the north-west of Capel Curig. This is the young river, looking south-east across its valley to the mountainous mass of Moel Siabod – 'moel' in Welsh meaning hill or mountain. *(Publisher unidentified)*

A similar view, closer to Moel Siabod, on a 1930-franked picturesque card overprinted with New Year's greetings. *(Wildt & Kray, London E.C.)*

Just west of Capel Curig the Llugwy is joined from the south-west by the Afon Nantygwryd (locally, simply Gwryd), via Llynnau Mymbyr (or the Mymbyr Lakes). This view is directly up the valley to the 3,560ft-high peak of Snowdon. The upper Llugwy is an ideal river for expert canoeists, the best access point perhaps being below the bridge at the Pen y Gwryd Hotel near its source. *("Picturesque North Wales" Raphael Tuck & Sons' "Oilette")*

A similar view across the lakes, this time as a real photograph rather than a gently romanticised oil painting. *(Valentine's)*

Llynnau Mymbyr from further east, looking down on the village of Capel Curig, with the A5 running up from the right. The old turnpike between Betws-y-Coed and Bangor ran through here, prompting the local estate owner Lord Penrhyn to build the inn seen in the centre distance; this became known as the Capel Curig Hotel – later the Royal Hotel – after the Shrewsbury–Holyhead mail coaches were rerouted along the road. *(Photochrom Co. Ltd., Tunbridge Wells)*

Looking towards the lakes again, with the Llugwy flowing from right to left in the foreground, joining the Nantygwryd on the far left. In the foreground is the old turnpike toll house. *(Publisher unidentified)*

Looking towards the rocky peak of Tryfan (3,010ft above sea level), south of the Llugwy to the west of Capel Curig. *(Judges' Ltd Hastings)*

One of a succession of minor bridges over the Llugwy, in Capel Curig . . . *(Scott Russell & Co., Art Publishers, Birmingham. "Scott" Series)*

Bridge, Capel Curig

. . . and a heavily romanticised painting of another. The standing man is sporting a large fishing rod – is he about to try his luck, or calling it a day? *(S Hildesheimer & Co, Ltd, London & Manchester)*

The Tyn-y-Coed Hotel in Capel Curig, on the A5 by Pont Cyfyng (see p. 50), and still very much in business today. In the 1877 *Gossiping Guide to Wales* this 'recently erected hotel with every modern improvement' advertised the fact that 'The Rivers and Lakes abound with excellent Trout.' *(Publisher unidentified)*

ROYAL HOTEL,
CAPEL CURIG.
First Class Family and Posting House.

Best Views in Wales. Good Fishing on all the Lakes, free of charge to Visitors staying at the Hotel. Boats may be used, free of charge.

Boats kept on the Capel Curig and Ogwen, this Hotel being nearest to the Ogwen.

GUIDES AND PONIES to Snowdon, Glydars, Moel Siabod, and Garnedd Llewelyn ; also conveyances to Llanberis, Beddgelert, Bangor, and Carnarvon.

All Orders by Post for Private Conveyances from the Royal Hotel, Capel Curig, to Bettws-y-Coed station are punctually attended to. **H. ROBERTS, Proprietor.**

TOUR No. 8.—By rail to Bettws-y-Coed, thence by coach to Capel Curig, ROYAL HOTEL, from the 11.2 a.m., 3.5 p.m., and 6 p.m., allowing time to see the Swallow and Cyffing Water Falls, returning the same day.

An advertisement for the Royal Hotel – the former Capel Curig Hotel – from the Ward, Lock & Co. Ltd *North Wales* guidebook of 1896, this time promising the possibility of boating as well as fishing. (Llyn Ogwen is just across the watershed from the Llugwy.) The author and traveller George Borrow wrote of the hotel, 'There I dined in a grand saloon amidst a great deal of fashionable company, who, probably conceiving from my heated and dusty appearance that I was some poor fellow travelling on foot from motives of economy, surveyed me with looks of the most suspicious disdain [. . .]'

An idyllic scene on the Llugwy in Capel Curig, below Cobden's Hotel – another of the hotels on this stretch of the A5 still open today. *("Grosvenor" Series)*

The Tan-y-Bwlch Hotel, another of Capel Curig's establishments built to serve the needs of travellers on what is now the A5, and also of course anglers and other visitors to the area. In the middle distance is the footbridge seen on p. 45. *(Valentine's Series)*

A 1909-franked postcard of the former parish church at Capel Curig, which grew from the thirteenth-century Curig's chapel, much enlarged over the years. A new St Curig's Church was built in the nineteenth century to cater for growing tourist numbers, and the older building rededicated to St Curig's mother, St Julitta. Deconsecrated in the 1970s, it is now maintained by the Friends of St Julitta. *(Valentine's Series)*

THE SNOWDONIA NATIONAL RECREATION CENTRE — CAPEL CURIG

The Snowdonia National Recreation Centre in Capel Curig – formerly the Royal Hotel, renamed Plas y Brenin. This whole region of North Wales is, today, very much a place for active leisure pursuits such as kayaking, cycling, mountaineering and so on, as opposed to the more genteel exercise undertaken by visitors a century or so ago. *(Hutton, 'Aldersyde', Llanelian, Colwyn Bay)*

A little downstream from Capel Curig, the Llugwy is crossed by the old Pont Cyfyng, or Cyfyng Bridge, carrying a minor road from the A5 south over the river. *(Valentine's Series)*

Just under 2 miles east of Capel Curig, immediately before the A5 crosses from the north bank of the Llugwy to the south, stands the dwelling known as Ty Hyll, or Ugly House, formerly used as overnight accommodation for drovers bringing cattle from north-west Wales down into England – notably the lush Shropshire plain – for fattening. *(St Albans Series)*

An old Cottage near Bettws-y-coed.

In contrast, a romanticised image of a cottage in the region – exact location unknown – on a 1910-franked postcard. In reality, such a dwelling would almost certainly have been cold, draughty and damp to live in, especially in a typical North Wales wet winter. *(Publisher unidentified)*

Snap-Shots of Welsh Scenery.   *Swallow Falls, Bettws-y-Coed.*

One of the famous attractions on the Llugwy, a little over halfway between Capel Curig and Betws-y-Coed, is the cataract known as the Swallow Falls – seen here on a 1911-franked, Saxony-printed postcard. *(Publisher unidentified)*

The Swallow Falls in full spate, by day . . . *(Valentine's)*

. . . and by night, although the photograph is almost certainly a heavily-doctored daytime one. *(The "D.F. & Co. Series". Delittle, Fenwick & Co., York)*

The next major attraction down the Llugwy from the Swallow Falls, and just outside Betws-y-Coed, is the Miners' Bridge, seen here from upstream. *(Frith's Series)*

The Miners' Bridge, from the south bank of the river, showing clearly the details of its wooden construction. It – or a predecessor – was built close to the site of a Roman ford to enable miners from the hamlet of Pentre-du, on the southern bank of the Llugwy, to cross it to work in the once-extensive lead mines in the Gwydyr Forest hills above the river. *(Lilywhite Ltd., Sowerby Bridge)*

The Miners' Bridge from downstream, with the Llugwy in full spate. *(The British Mirror Series)*

While stereoscopic photos, looked at on a special viewer, were popular Victorian and Edwardian novelties with many surviving into the present, smaller stereoscopic postcards of that period are rare. These also required a hand-held viewer in order for their full 3D effect to be achieved and appreciated, which meant that the market for them was a comparatively limited one. *(Publisher unidentified)*

Downstream from the Miners' Bridge is an old stone bridge at Pont-y-Pair, on the western edge of Betws-y-Coed. The view here is across the Llugwy to the A5 on the south bank of the river. *(Sepiatone Series The Photochrom Co., Ltd., London and Tunbridge Wells)*

Pont-y-Pair means 'Bridge of the Cauldron' in honour of the swirling waters below it. In contrast, above the bridge is the Still Pool where the Llugwy briefly calms before making its sudden descent. *(S. Hildesheimer & Co., Ldt. [sic] London & Manchester)*

Between the Still Pool and the bridge is the rocky islet known as Fir Tree Island – or in the past, as here, simply Fir Island. The origin of both versions of the name is self-explanatory. *(The Wrench Series)*

Fir Tree Island again, from above the bridge . . . *(Valentine & Sons, Ltd., Dundee & London)*

. . . and looking downstream, on a 1907-franked card. *(Frith's Series F. Frith & Co. Ltd. Reigate)*

Pont-y-Pair, on a short succession of postcards selected to show how different publishers treated the same subject. Firstly, a coloured German-printed card. *(Hartmann)*

Secondly, another LNWR official issue card, posted in 1906, this time printed as a black and white photograph. *(London & North Western Railway Company)*

Thirdly, another close-up of the main arch of the bridge, on a 1912-franked card showing
what appears to be a club or school outing crossing over. *(BR Ltd)*

Lastly, looking upstream past the bridge, with the tops of the Fir Tree Island trees visible above the parapet in the centre. *(Salmon Series J. Salmon, Sevenoaks, England)*

The view from the bridge, looking upstream to Fir Tree Island again, this time with the river running high. *(Photochrom Co. Ltd., London and Tunbridge Wells)*

The Pont-y-Pair Hotel, by the bridge, on another Saxony-printed card. *(Stewart & Woolf, London, E.C.)*

Below Pont-y-Pair the Llugwy turns abruptly northwards before flowing under the railway branch line to join the Afon Conwy. The beginning of this change of direction is first evident here, as is the river's now more peaceful nature. *(The "Dainty" Series)*

Meeting of the Waters, Bettws-y-Coed

Where the two rivers meet, the Llugwy flowing northwards in from the bottom of the picture and the Conwy flowing from east to west (right to left) before turning north again down its valley. *(Valentine's Series)*

Finally, three views of the Conwy immediately below Betws-y-Coed. Firstly, looking back to the town on a coloured photographic postcard . . . *(C.W. Faulkner & Co. Ltd., London, E.C. 1)*

. . . and secondly, a similar but romanticised view, this time printed from an artist's painting. *(S Hildesheimer & Co., Ltd, London & Manchester. Views of North Wales)*

Lastly, the view back southwards to the mountains around Betws-y-Coed again, on a charming real photograph of children swimming in the river. *(Raphael Tuck & Sons "Silverette" Bettws-y-Coed Series II)*

5

The Lower River

This was the Dyffryn Conway, the celebrated Vale of Conway, to which in the summer time fashionable gentry from all parts of Britain resort for shade and relaxation.

(Wild Wales, George Borrow, 1857)

(Sepiatone Series The Photochrom Co., Ltd., London and Tunbridge Wells)

The tranquil Conwy below Betws-y-Coed, the river now deep enough for small pleasure boats. (*Photochrom Co., Ltd. Graphic Studios – Tunbridge Wells – Kent*)

Three miles down the Conwy, the first sizeable settlement below Betws-y-Coed is reached at Llanrwst, a wool market town named after the sixth-century St Grwst. This general view across the valley, from west to east, shows the town on the rising ground beyond the river. (*Valentine's "Selectype" Series*)

Llanrwst Church, picturesquely situated on the east bank of the Conwy. Founded in 1170, the church of St Grwst was rebuilt in 1470 and extensively restored in 1884; in its Gwydir Chapel is the stone coffin of Llywelyn the Great. *(The Photochrom Co. Ltd. London and Tunbridge Wells)*

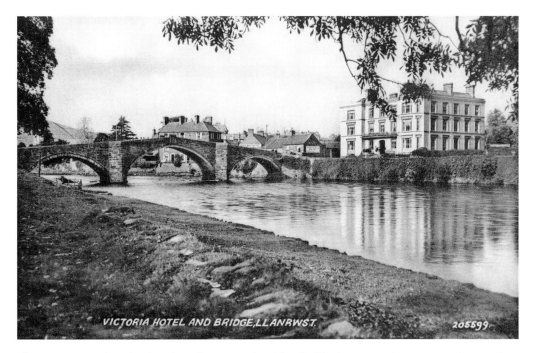

The most eye-catching landmark in Llanrwst is the old arched bridge across the river, seen here with its close neighbour the Victoria Hotel built to cash-in on the coming of the railway. *("Sepiatype" Postcard Valentine & Sons Ltd., Dundee and London)*

A closer view of the bridge. Reputedly designed by the architect Inigo Jones, the three-arch stone structure was erected in 1636 on the orders of Sir John Wynne of Gwydir Castle. *(R.J. Jones, The Library. Llanrwst)*

Looking down on Llanrwst Bridge from a vantage point in the Victoria Hotel, on a 1923-franked postcard, with its minor road heading off across the Conwy's flood plain to the mountains beyond. *(The Wrench Series)*

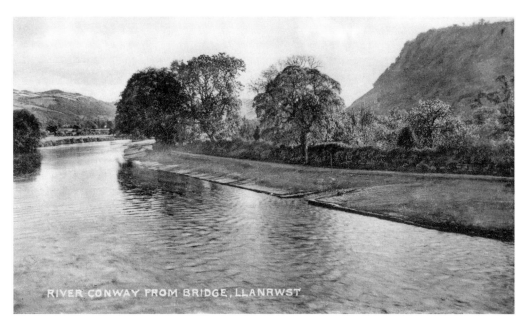

The view upstream from the bridge, on a 1935-franked card. The steep sides of the valley make an impressive frame for the scene. *(Valentine's "Selectype" Series)*

Station Road, Llanrwst, in the days when the horse and cart still ruled the roads. Llanrwst station was opened in 1863 by the LNWR and, after being replaced in 1868 when the branch line was extended to Betws-y-Coed, has served the town ever since. *(The Wrench Series)*

A charmingly posed rustic scene in Gwydyr Woods, just across the river bridge from Llanrwst, probably photographed in Edwardian times. *(L. Williams & Sons, Carrington House, Llanrwst)*

The minor road over Llanrwst Bridge, seen on pp. 67 and 68, takes the visitors to Gwydir Castle, a nineteenth-century mansion built around a fourteenth-century hall (extended in the sixteenth century). In Tudor and Stuart times it was the home of the Wynne family, and is still in private ownership today. *(The L.P. & F.A.P. Llandrindod Wells)*

The dining room in Gwydir Castle where Charles I and his queen, Henrietta Maria, are reputed to have dined. *(Valentine's Series)*

In the formal gardens at Gwydir Castle, on a 1909-franked card. *(The Wrench Series)*

High in the hills to the west of Gwydir Castle is Llyn Geirionydd, a lake which, together with Llyn Crafnant (see below), feeds water into the Conwy via the Afon Crafnant. The Bard Taliesin is said to have been born on the shore here. *(Valentine's Series)*

Llyn Crafnant, Llyn Geirionydd's companion to its west in the heart of lead-mining country, today used as a reservoir. *(Sepiatone Series The Photochrom Co., Ltd., London and Tunbridge Wells)*

Almost exactly the same view as on the previous postcard, only this time rendered as a night-time painting. The sender's message is, simply, 'With the best of Xmas Wishes – Xmas 1905.' *(S. Hildesheimer & Co., Ltd. London & Manchester)*

Immediately below Llanrwst the Conwy swings away from its steep, eastern valley to cross the flood plain to the equally steep western side of its valley at Trefriw, roughly 11 miles above Conwy. Here the Afon Crafnant – complete with its own Fairy Glen – joins the river. *(The Wrench Series)*

FAIRY FALLS, TREFRIW 107

No Welsh beauty spot, with a young river in a bosky gorge, would be complete without a Fairy Glen and, as the previous card proves, the Crafnant is no exception. The Fairy Falls, captured here on this 1908-franked card, are a bonus and add greatly to the glen's charms. In the nineteenth century the falls powered a mill making hammers and chisels; today the waters generate electricity to power a weaving mill in Trefriw. *(Grosvenor Series. W.A. & S.S.)*

Trefriw, now as in the 1920s when this postcard was probably published, is essentially a one-street village, its main thoroughfare . . . *(Valentine's Series)*

. . . being a minor road that hugs the western side of the Conwy, squeezed between the river and the valley side. Once part of the mail coach route to Ireland, the road was rendered redundant by the opening of the Waterloo Bridge at Betws-y-Coed, which made for a much shorter route to Bangor and Holyhead. *(Grosvenor Series W.A. & S.S.)*

An advertisement for the Bellevue Hotel in Trefriw, highlighting the attractions of the district. (Note the connection with the Castle Hotel in Conwy – see p. 100.) This establishment is now the Princes Arms Hotel and its guests now arrive by road rather than by the river. This advertisement was taken from Ward, Lock & Co. Ltd's 1896 *North Wales* guidebook.

During the late-Victorian/Edwardian era, Trefriw was the highest point on the Conwy that could be reached by medium-sized pleasure boats. Here there was a small quay on an artificial inlet off the river that was once an important river port – especially for ore from the Gwydyr Forest mines – but since the late nineteenth century almost exclusively a landing place for tourists, of which up to 1,000 could arrive daily. *(The Wrench Series)*

The quayside inlet at Trefriw, looking northwards towards the Conwy, on a 1909-franked postcard. *(The L.P. & F.A.P. Llandrindod Wells)*

Looking northwards across the quay again, with two Conwy steamers plying their trade, on a card presumably posted in 1906. Below Trefriw the river is tidal, and the steamers needed high water to come this far up the river. *(Peacock Brand)*

The quayside viewed from across the river. The 1908 sender's message reads, 'Still here – and enjoying life hugely.' Navigation to Trefriw on the former scale ended in the 1930s, a victim of the silting-up of the river caused in part by the construction of Telford's road bridge at Conwy and by the growing popularity of wider-ranging motor coach excursions. *(BR Ltd)*

Trefriw quayside again, this time with two paddle steamers, and one other craft, in attendance. Part of the quayside still exists and can be explored from the riverbank footpath. *(Grosvenor Series. W.A. & S.S.)*

A 1909-franked postcard of a busy scene at Trefriw with a small paddle steamer – the *St George* – by the quay and a screw-driven vessel alongside, both craft apparently with a full complement of passengers. *(Publisher unidentified)*

Looking northwards down the Conwy Valley – or Vale of Conway as it was more poetically known – from above the quayside (just out of picture, bottom right). The sender's message, from 1917, reads, 'Mother and I came along this beautiful River this morning by Steamer to Trefriw. Then we walked some distance towards Bettws. Then we got a lift.' *(T.R. Hammond, Conway)*

Less than a mile below Trefriw is Trefriw Wells, where the presence of a chalybeate spring (known to the Romans) led to attempts in the eighteenth and nineteenth centuries to market the site as a spa. According to the legend on the reverse of the card, the spring had, 'The richest Sulphur-Iron Waters known; wonderfully efficacious for Anaemia, Indigestion, Rheumatism, Insomnia, Neuritis, Debility, etc.' Other, more neutral sources say the taste was quite disgusting! *(Publisher unidentified)*

Below Trefriw the broadening Conwy begins to meander across its flood plain with the next settlement of any size being the village of Tal-y-Cafn on the eastern bank. It is seen here to the right of its river bridge, centre picture, on this 1917-franked card written aboard the river steamer *King George*. *(T.R. Hammond, Conway)*

The Ferry Hotel at Tal-y-Cafn, with a paddle steamer and another craft moored up. This was one of the stopping points on the river cruises – much to the benefit of the hotel's trade. *(Publisher unidentified)*

Looking downriver from the Ferry Hotel. The proprietor's name is given on the previous card as
W. Davies, though whether he published or merely sold souvenir postcards is uncertain. *(Grosvenor Series
W.A. & S.S.)*

Another card from the same publisher, this time showing the road approach – off the A470 – to the Ferry
Hotel. *(Grosvenor Series W.A. & S., S.)*

The view upstream at Tal-y-Cafn with the Ferry Hotel on the far left and the rather ornate river bridge in the centre. The 1916 sender of this postcard, Bert, has written, rather ungraciously, to Mary in London, 'Have been to a Welsh service this morning. Very nice but I could not understand it of course. It is the most abominable language you could ever wish to hear.' *(T.R. Hammond, Conway)*

The bridge at Tal-y-Cafn, seen from the opposite bank of the Conwy. The minor road off to the right leads to the village of Tyn-y-Groes. *(Valentine's)*

In the woods above Tyn-y-Groes, with one of the many minor tributaries of the Afon Conwy tumbling down to meet it. *(Publisher unidentified)*

Another of the many minor tributaries of the Conwy, this time destined to join it at Tal-y-Cafn – not the poor attempt at spelling the place name correctly! *("Weekly Tale-Teller" Post Card. printed by Delittle, Fenwick & Co., York)*

Below Tal-y-Cafn, looking upstream on a 1909-franked card to the bridge – and beyond that, to the mountains of Snowdonia. On the left bank, the road and railway to Betws-y-Coed are forced, by the encroaching hillside, to the very edge of the river. *(Publisher unidentified)*

Below Tal-y-Cafn, again on the east bank of the river, is Bodnant Hall and its famous gardens. The hall – seen here on a Berlin-printed postcard – was constructed in about 1790 and later enlarged, though the present garden dates from 1875. *(The Lonsdale Series)*

The Lily Terrace at Bodnant Hall. The garden – generally acknowledged to be one of the most spectacular in the world and since 1949 in the care of the National Trust – was laid out by the Lancashire industrialist Henry Pochin and extended by his daughter, wife of the first Lord Aberconwy. *(Valentine's)*

Another of the splendours of Bodnant is the wonderful Italian Garden, again on the upper level above the wilder and less formal wooded slopes beside the river below. *(Valentine's)*

The view south-westwards across the Conwy below Bodnant. This is a popular spot for bird watchers, especially at low tide when the mud flats are revealed and waders, heron and shelduck flock here to feed. *(Grosvenor Series W.A. & S., S.)*

The delightful Glan Conwy, on the eastern side of the river a little to the south of Conwy and its river bridges, and the site of both an old ford and the first station along the branch from Llandudno Junction on the main Chester to Holyhead railway line. *(John Roberts, Post Office, Glan Conway)*

At the town of Conwy another tributary of the river, the Afon Gyffin, joins it almost beneath the road and rail bridges, at a spot known as Benarth Conwy, complete with its own tiny quayside as photographed for this 1915-franked postcard. *(Frith's Series, F. Frith & Co., Ltd at their Reigate Works)*

6

Conwy Town

This ancient and most picturesque town is situated on the sloping side of the vale through which the river of the same name flows. The town and castle are entirely surrounded by walls, which, being of rude triangular form, are not unlike the outline of a Welsh harp.

(The Official Tourists' Picturesque Guide, London & North Western Railway Co., 1876)

(W. Shaw, Burslem)

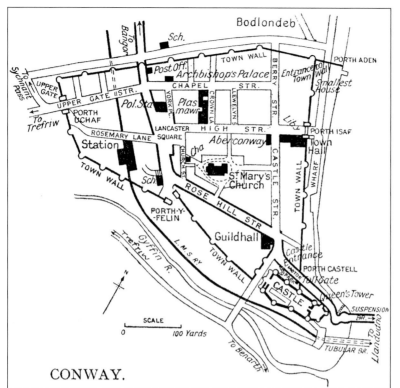

A map of Conwy, showing its streets and landmarks, as printed in a Ward, Lock & Co. Ltd *Guide to Colwyn Bay and North Wales* of the 1950s.

A 1953-franked postcard with a pull-out strip of eight small photographs of Conwy and district. Welsh ladies, taking tea or spinning wool, were a popular subject for postcard publishers, though the cards were not usually overprinted, as here, with a specific place name. *(Valentine's "Mail Novelty" Post Card)*

The approach to Conwy from the south, on a 1945-franked card. The town is situated on the west bank of the river, just visible immediately to the right beyond the castle. *(A. Vass, Glanafon Stores, Gyffin, Conway)*

Approaching closer to the castle, from the same direction, on a 1958-franked card. The present structure is what remains of Edward I's great stronghold of the 1280s. On the right are the twin portals to the tubular railway bridge over the Conwy. *(Publisher unidentified)*

SECTION OF TOWN WALL FROM CYFFIN ROAD CONWAY.

The back, or landward, side of Conwy Castle again, with a surviving section of the town's former defensive wall to the fore. The wall stretches for some 1,400yds and was constructed at the same time as the castle, to an average height of 30ft – just one of the reasons why the town is designated a World Heritage Site. *(Publisher unidentified)*

One of the surviving entrances into the walled town, Porth-y-Felin (Mill Gate in English) on the southern side of the town, looking from Rose Hill Street through its arch to the river below. *(Peacock "Stylochrom" Post Card. The Pictorial Stationery Co., Ltd., London)*

Two more of Conwy's gateways: this is Porth Uchaf, or Upper Gate, on the landward side of the
town at the end of Uppergate Street . . . *(Publisher unidentified)*

Porth Isaf, Conway.

. . . and this is Porth Isaf, or Lower Gate, on the opposite side of the town at the foot of the High Street, giving access to the river. *(Publisher unidentified)*

The oldest house in Conwy is thought to be the building known as Aberconwy, on the corner of Castle Street and the High Street, captured here on a 1919-franked postcard. It is a rare surviving example of a fourteenth-century timber and stone merchant's house, with an external staircase. *(Sepiatone Series The Photochrom Co. Ltd. London and Tunbridge Wells)*

Aberconwy again, this time on a rather later but still pre-Second World War card. The house dates from about 1500 but has been much altered and restored over the years, both internally and, as can be seen in this sequence of images, externally. Its name means simply 'Mouth of the Conwy'. *(Publisher unidentified)*

An even later photograph of Aberconwy, showing its timber framing now covered with a render of some kind. Once there would have been a number of such houses in the town, the homes of well-to-do merchants and the like, but they have largely gone or been modernised beyond recognition. *(G. Leonard Bean Ltd., 52 Brook Street, Chester)*

Aberconwy at an earlier date, on a German-printed card – Germany, and Saxony in particular, was an important supplier of postcards to the British market. The caption records its nineteenth-century conversion into a temperance hotel. *(Baur's Series)*

Two interior views of Aberconwy: the restored kitchen . . . *(Publisher unidentified)*

. . . and the restored dining room. Note the wide variation in age attributed to the house over these last three cards! The house is now in the care of the National Trust and is open to the public. *(Publisher unidentified)*

Plas Mawr. (A.D. 1585). Conway.

Another of Conwy's old buildings is Plas Mawr, or Great Hall or Mansion, on the corner of the High Street and Crown Lane. It was built by Robert Wynne of Gwydir Castle between 1577 and 1580 as his smaller town house, later passing into the hands of the Mostyn family. *(Publisher unidentified)*

Plas Mawr again, on a typical Welsh souvenir postcard complete with a border of leeks and Prince of Wales' feathers aimed squarely at the mass tourist market. The ornate stonework of the gables and chimneys on the house are typical of its Tudor period. *(Valentine's Series)*

Inside Plas Mawr: the formal reception room with its ornate plasterwork ceiling. E.R. (for Elizabeth Regina) can be seen above the fireplace flanking the royal arms supported by the English lion and the Welsh dragon. *(T.R. Hammond)*

Outside Plas Mawr: the typical Elizabethan town house courtyard and entrance steps at the rear of the building. The house, home to the Royal Cambrian Academy of Art (now housed behind it) from 1885 to 1994, is in the care of Cadw. *(Peacock Series "Platino-Photo" Postcard. Pictorial Stationery Co., Ltd. London)*

THE
CASTLE HOTEL,
CONWAY,

Is the Most Central in North Wales,

For all Tourists wishing to visit its

RENOWNED SCENERY.

—————

FIRST CLASS. ELEGANTLY FURNISHED.
EVERY MODERN CONVENIENCE.

—————

BEST GOLF LINKS IN WALES, AND FACING THE SEA.

Spacious Coffee Room, Ladies' Drawing Room, Bath Room, Billiards, Posting, &c.

Miss DUTTON, Proprietress.

An advertisement for the Castle Hotel in Conwy High Street, extolling the comforts and amenities expected of a certain class of hotel of that period. Still in business today, this former coaching inn is made up of two old hostelries, the Castle and the King's Head, built on the site of a Cistercian abbey. From Ward, Lock & Co. Ltd's 1896 *North Wales* guidebook. (See also p. 76.)

The Smallest House in Wales.

Another of Conwy's old buildings – and perhaps, after the castle, its most famous – is the dwelling popularly known as 'the smallest house in Wales', one in a terrace of houses on the quayside. *(BR Ltd)*

The frontage of the smallest house again, this time on a real photographic postcard, showing the tourist trappings of prominent signage and the obligatory lady in Welsh costume. The notice above the door announces an admission price of *2d. (Publisher unidentified)*

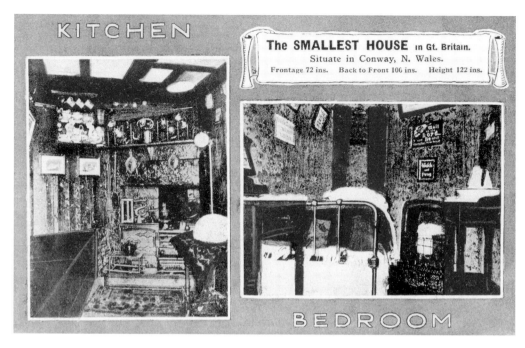

A two-view card of the smallest house's interior, showing its two tiny rooms: the kitchen/living room downstairs and the bedroom upstairs. *(Mrs E. Williams, 11, Lowergate Street, Conway)*

In the graveyard of Conwy's parish church, St Mary's, lies a well-known grave, famous for being immortalised by William Wordsworth in his sentimental poem 'We Are Seven'. The church is the most substantial remnant of the town's late twelfth-century Cistercian abbey, granted a charter by Llywelyn the Great in 1198. *(Mr. Moody, Bangor Road, Conway)*

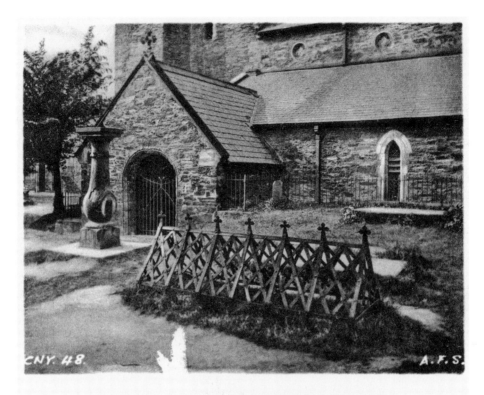

THE GRAVE IMMORTALIZED BY WORDSWORTH'S POEM
"WE ARE SEVEN"
AND OLD SUNDIAL, CONWAY CHURCHYARD.

I met a little cottage girl;
  She was eight years old, she said;
Her hair was thick with many a curl
  That clustered round her head.

"Sisters and brothers, little maid
  How many may you be?"
"How many? Seven in all," she said,
  And wondering, looked at me.

"And where are they, I pray you tell?"
  She answered, "Seven are we;
And two of us at Conway dwell
  And two are gone to sea.

"Two of us in the churchyard lie,
  My sister and my brother,
And in the churchyard cottage I
  Dwell near them with my mother."

"You say that two at Conway dwell
  And two are gone to sea,
Yet ye are seven! - I pray you tell,
  Sweet maid, how this may be?"

"Their graves are green and may be seen,"
  The little maid replied,
"Twelve steps or more from my mother's door,
  And they are side by side.

"My stockings there I sometimes knit,
  My kerchief there I hem;
And there upon the ground I sit,
  And sing a song to them.

"And often after sunset, Sir,
  When it is light and fair.
I take my little porringer
  And eat my supper there."

"How many are you then," said I,
  "If they two are in heaven?"
Quick was the little maid's reply,
  "O master! we are seven."

"But they are dead; those two are dead!
  Their spirits are in heaven!"
'Twas throwing words away, for still
  The little maid would have her will:
"NAY, MASTER! WE ARE SEVEN!"

A long extract from Wordsworth's poem, beneath a photo of the grave, though without the addition of a posed child as in the previous card. Note the iron cage over the grave, literally a safeguard against body-snatchers, and the imposing sundial on the left. *(Frith's Series F. Frith & Co., Ltd., Reigate)*

A very slightly saucy Edwardian postcard proclaiming the 'natural Beauties' to be found in Conwy – a far cry indeed from today's crude examples. *(B.B. London Series)*

On to Conwy Castle, the town's crowning glory, here seen from the landward (and least prepossessing) side. *(Postcard Picture Judges Ltd. Hastings)*

Moving round the skirting walls, this is the main entrance into the castle complex. Construction of the castle was begun in 1283, as part of Edward I's grand plan to subjugate the Welsh following the death of Prince Llywelyn. *(Baur's Series)*

Inside the main building of the castle, with the remains of one of the two banqueting halls (there was a king's and a queen's) to the fore. The architect was James of St George, or Master of the King's Works, to give him his official title. *(T.R. Hammond, Conway)*

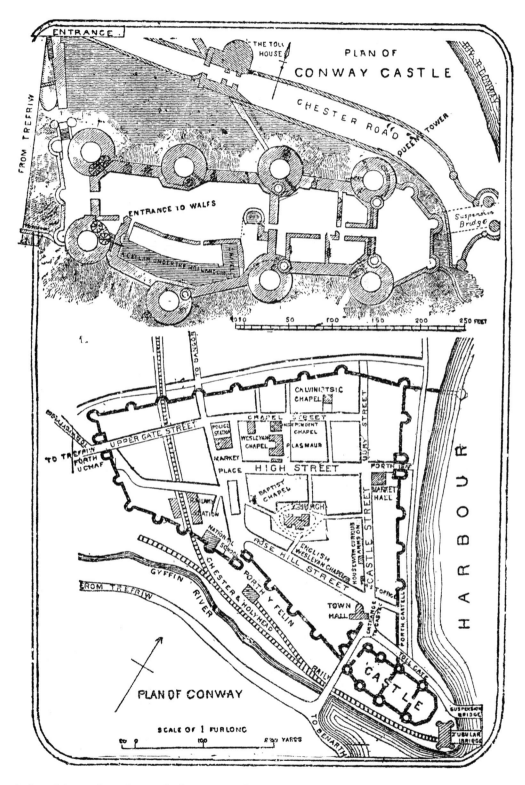

A plan of the castle, with its eight drum towers designed to give defenders a wide field of fire, and the old town walls, from an early twentieth-century *Gossiping Guide to Wales*.

Conway Castle, Queen Eleanor's Chapel.

The remains of Queen Eleanor's Chapel in the castle, named after the wife of Edward I and perhaps reserved exclusively for her private devotions. *(T.R. Hammond)*

Conway Castle and Bridge

Looking to the castle from the east, with Thomas Telford's 1824–6 suspension road bridge paralleled by Robert Stephenson's tubular railway bridge of 1846–9 behind it. This was the ancient site of a ferry, displaced by Telford's bridge following the call for such a structure to be built after thirteen people lost their lives when the Irish Mail coach toppled off the ferry on Christmas Day 1806. *(Valentine's Series)*

Telford's bridge, on a 1906-franked card, with a Conwy fisherman beached on the shore beneath it. Above him, a new walkway has been added onto the side of the bridge, a move necessitated by the growing volume of vehicular traffic passing over it. *(B.R. Ltd)*

A somewhat later view of the bridge, this time with a motor cruiser beneath it, showing in greater detail the new walkway. Telford's design deliberately echoes the medieval architecture of the castle, and serves to compliment rather than detract from it. *(Valentine's "Photo-Brown" Series)*

The eastern approach to Telford's bridge, on a 1914-franked postcard, with the anchoring points for the two massive suspension chains in the foreground. The decking of the bridge is suspended from these chains, rather than being supported from below, hence the name for this type of structure. It is similar in design to Telford's 1819–26 bridge across the Menai Strait from near Bangor to Anglesey. *(G.R. Thompson, The Post Card King, Llandudno)*

Looking past the castle from the west, with Stephenson's railway bridge on the right. *(Bunney's Ltd., Liverpool & Llandudno)*

An artist's impression of the construction of the railway bridge, on an official 1905 LNWR postcard. The two metal tubes carrying the railway tracks were assembled on shore, floated out on the river, then jacked into position. Stephenson's flash of genius was realising that, being rigid box sections, the tubes would not need supporting other than at each end, meaning that no central (and very expensive) pillars would have to be built in the river. *(L.N.W.R. Additional Series)*

Another 1905 LNWR postcard, this time showing the western entrance to the railway bridge, hard by the walls of the castle. Stephenson repeated his pioneering design on his longer Britannia Bridge over the Menai Strait which, when opened in 1850, filled the last gap in the railway line between Chester and Holyhead. *(L.N.W.R. Additional Series)*

By the 1950s the sheer volume of traffic on the A55 along the North Wales coast meant that a new road crossing of the Conwy was required, and in 1958 a second road bridge was opened (and Telford's bridge, now in the care of the National Trust, closed to vehicles). Three decades later the exact same problem led to the opening, in 1991, of a road tunnel laid on the bed of the estuary below the (now bypassed) town as part of the upgrading of the A55 to a dual carriageway. *(Valentine's)*

7

Into the Bay

"Begin at the beginning," the King said, very gravely, "and go on till you come to the end: then stop."

(Alice's Adventures in Wonderland, Lewis Carroll, 1865)

(Valentine's)

Below the bridges the fresh waters of the Afon Conwy continue on towards the salt waters of Conwy Bay though, rather unusually, the mouth of the estuary narrows sharply, constricted over the centuries by material gradually being forced eastwards by wind and tide along the coast. *(R.E. Jones & Bros., Conway)*

Looking back towards Conwy Castle and the bridges, from Marine Walk on the western side of the estuary. *(Valentine's)*

A similar but earlier (franked in 1913) view showing the age-old use made of this stretch of the estuary, by the town's inhabitants, as a sheltered haven for their boats. *(SPC State Series, Liverpool)*

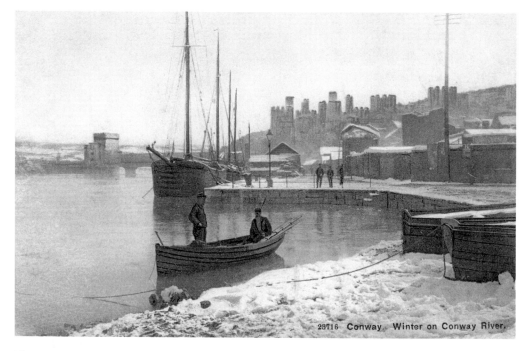

The scene in winter, on a 1908-franked card, with the ancient masonry of the quayside clearly delineated by the snow. According to one version of the Welsh legend, it was from this spot that the (possibly) mythical Prince Madog set sail to discover North America in the year 1170 – a tale taken up by the Tudors in a later century to bolster their territorial claims to that continent. *(Photochrom Co., Ltd., London)*

The view back from out in the estuary, amid the local fishing fleet. The quayside is directly below the castle on the right. *(E.T.W. Dennis & Sons, Ltd. London & Scarboro')*

The view from the shore of the estuary across to the town of Deganwy, with the long, low line of its slate wharf on the right, on a 1920s-franked postcard. *(Exclusive Celesque Series, Photochrom Co. Ltd. London and Tunbridge Wells)*

A similar view, on a 1909-franked card, with one of the Conwy paddle steamers berthed at the landing stage (made up of the old hulls of former sailing ships). The outer section of the walkway is hinged, allowing it to rise and fall with the tide while remaining connected to the boat. *(Frith's Series F. Frith & Co. Ltd. Reigate)*

The 'beach' at Conwy – or more correctly, the shingly shore – further down the estuary, looking towards its narrow mouth. *(O. Evans, Photographer, Conway)*

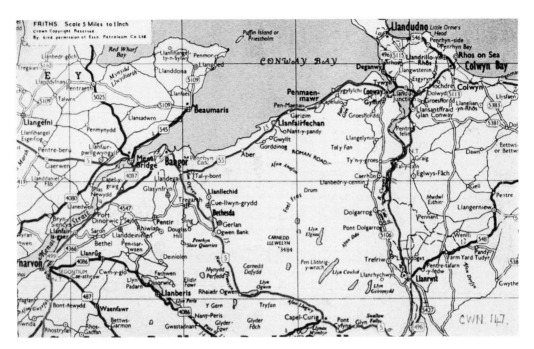

A map card of the Conwy and Conwy Bay. Souvenir postcards featuring maps are still produced today, though nowadays they are almost always hand-drawn with added vignettes of local landmarks on a colourful background, rather than the atlas extract, printed in plain sepia, of this example. *(Frith's Series F. Frith & Co., Ltd., Reigate)*

Looking almost due north across the estuary to Deganwy. Just creeping into shot on the left is the area known as the Beacons, at the end of the river mouth sand spit, on the edge of a golf course. *(Lancaster & Co., Deganwy)*

Conway Morfa Camp & Deganwy.

The flat land housing the golf course between the Beacons and the ancient cliff-line is Conwy Morfa ('morfa' meaning moor or marsh). From the late nineteenth century until after the First World War this was also the site of a large military training camp for volunteer battalions, complete with its own station on the main Chester–Holyhead railway line in the foreground. Several of the cards reproduced here are franked as having been posted to families and friends from in the camp. *(Hammond's Series, Conway)*

Conway from Deganwy.

15729

Moving down and across the estuary, this is the view back to Conwy from Deganwy as printed on a 1959-franked card, with the Conwy's fishing boats displaced by leisure craft. The sender has written, 'Having a very nice holiday with glorious weather, we are all feeling the effects of sunburn.' *(J. Salmon Ltd., Sevenoaks)*

Deganwy Castle Hotel, on another postcard sent (to Rochdale) by someone having 'splendid weather' – not the general English perception of the prevailing climate in North Wales but actually very often the case. The seventeenth-century listed hotel takes its name from the ruins of the castle built by the Earl of Chester in 1211 (on the site of an earlier Norman fortress), which once commanded this side of the bay – the name Deganwy derives from Dinas Conwy, or 'fortress on the Conwy'. *(The Lancaster Series, Deganwy)*

Looking down on Deganwy from the heights of Gannock Park. Across the river is Conwy Morfa while on the right the exposed sandbank shows just how tricky the entrance to the estuary can be for sailors. The sender of this 1920-franked card has also remarked that, 'To-day has been very hot.' *(Lancaster & Co., Deganwy)*

The view from Deganwy up the estuary with the end of the old slate wharf on the right. In the distance, the extent of the causeway carrying the road and rail links to the Conwy bridges is clearly apparent on this 1930-franked postcard. *(Valentine's)*

A fuller view of the slate wharf, on a 1918-franked card. Constructed by the LNWR in 1882, the wharf was used for trans-shipping slate, brought down the Conwy Valley by rail from Blaenau Ffestiniog, onto ocean-going vessels for export all around the world. *(J.E. Jones, Ye Old Post Office Stores, Deganwy)*

Two views of Deganwy from the opposite shore. Firstly, on a 1900s postcard showing one of the river paddle steamers against a backdrop of local sailing club boats . . . *(B.R. Ltd)*

. . . and on a similar vintage card, with a sailing club regatta in full swing. The sender's somewhat strange message reads, 'According to the name this place seems to be in Wales.' *(The Wrench Series)*

A 1950s postcard of the promenade at Deganwy, a quiet little town overshadowed by its bigger (and perhaps brasher) neighbouring resorts along the North Wales coast. *(Photochrom Co., Ltd. Graphic Studios – Tunbridge Wells – Kent)*

In contrast, much the same scene more than thirty years earlier, on a 1921-franked postcard. The sender notes that, 'The weather is behaving itself once more.' *(Valentine's Series)*

Beyond Deganwy lies an expanse of golf links, and beyond them, Llandudno. Although the greater portion of that town is outside the scope of this volume, its West Shore is very much part of Conwy Bay, the eastern and northern limits of which are marked by the Great Orme headland, seen here on this 1916-franked card of the model yacht pond. *(Carbofoto Series G.R. Thompson, 63A. Mostyn Street, Llandudno)*

The West Shore's famous Lewis Carroll Memorial by F.W. Forrester, unveiled by Lloyd George in 1933, commemorating the author's visit to Dean Liddell on holiday here, and his walks on the sands with Liddell's daughter Alice – the inspiration for the *Alice* books. It is said that this expanse of beach gave rise to the lines, 'The Walrus and the Carpenter, Were walking close at hand. They wept like anything to see, Such quantities of sand: "If this were only cleared away," They said, "it would be grand!"' *(Salmon Series J. Salmon Ltd., Sevenoaks)*

The "Lewis Carroll" Memorial, West Shore, Llandudno.

A gold-edged, 1939-franked postcard of the Carroll Memorial in close-up with, at the top, the unmistakable figure of the White Rabbit from *Alice's Adventures in Wonderland*. Sadly for Carroll enthusiasts, there is no firm evidence that Carroll ever visited Llandudno at all. *(Publisher unidentified)*

Entrance to Marine Drive, West Shore, Llandudno.

At the northern end of the West Shore is the exit from the Marine Drive, the narrow roadway round the Great Orme cut out of the cliff face in 1879. (The entrance – the road is one-way – is on the other side of the headland, by the pier.) This 1914-franked card dates from the time when visitors were driven round it in hired horse-brakes . . . *(Valentine's X.L. Series)*

TOLL GATE, WEST SHORE,
LLANDUDNO.

. . . while this one, from a decade or so later, shows that motor vehicles had taken over this duty. *(Publisher unidentified)*

The end of our journey: the northern extremity of the Great Orme, with its lighthouse and, just below the skyline, the scar of the Marine Drive. *("Pictorchrom" Post Card. The Pictorial Stationery Co. Ltd., London)*

Looking back down from the Great Orme over the West Shore and the grand sweep of Conwy Bay, with the mountains of Snowdonia looming impressively in the far distance. *(English Series Photo-Precision Ltd., St. Albans)*

A final look at the timeless Conwy, on a 1907-franked postcard. The sender – Albert – wishes the recipient – a Miss Day – 'Many happy returns of the day,' it being a common practice in a less commercialised age to use postcards to send birthday greetings. Truly a felicitous note on which to end our journey down this delightful river. *(E.S. London)*